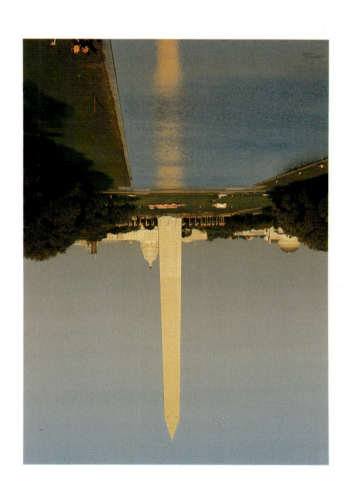

WASHING

Published by
Gallery Books
A Division of W.H. Smith Publishers Inc.
112 Madison Avenue
New York, New York 10016
USA.

Produced by
Bison Books Corp.
15 Sherwood Place,
Greenwich, CT. 06830
USA.

ISBN 0-8317-9307-4

Printed in Hong Kong

2 3 4 5 6 7 8 9 10

TON D.C.

TEXT THOMAS G AYLESWORTH
VIRGINIA L AYLESWORTH

DESIGN MIKE ROSE

GALLERY BOOKS
An imprint of W.H. Smith Publishers Inc.
112 Madison Avenue
New York, New York 10016

A Bison Book

Maryland and Virginia—and Washington chose a French engineer, Major Pierre Charles L'Enfant, to survey the land and lay out the city. In 1791 L'Enfant set up his planning headquarters in a small stone cottage in the nearby town of Georgetown.

L'Enfant's vision was big and beautiful—great avenues, expansive parks and at least one boulevard a full 400 feet wide. Plans were progressing nicely and buildings were rising (Washington himself laid the Capitol cornerstone in 1792) when Major L'Enfant's enthusiasm for spaciousness ran away with him. He demanded that a wealthy District citizen move his impressive home out of the path of an onrushing boulevard, and, after the angry words that ensued, Washington was forced to ask for the Major's resignation.

Still, present-day Washington owes much of its beauty to the young Frenchman. The basic concept was his, but preserving it has not been easy. For one thing, not all heads of government have shared L'Enfant' reverence for clear-spaced grandeur. Andrew Jackson, for example, is rumored to have planted the great gray Treasury Building directly in the way of a planned White House-Capitol vista with an arbitrary wave of his cane.

For another, government buildings have suffered chronic lack-of-funds construction stoppages. Though work on the capital began in 1792, the permanent cast-iron dome was not in place for Lincoln's 1861 Inaugural,

Preface

There are literally hundreds of cities all over the world that call themselves unique, but Washington DC is the only one that truly deserves that appellation. It is the first city that was created with the distinct purpose of establishing a home for a nation's government.

As early as 1783, even before that magnificent experiment on democratic government—the United States of America—came into being, the Continental Congress decided to set up a federal city as a permanent site for its meetings, but the issue of slavery made it difficult to choose a location. Slave-owning Southerners opposed Philadelphia as a site for the capital, because the Quakers of that city opposed slavery and favored abolition. Northerners did not want Congress to meet in a slave-holding area because they felt that it might seem that the United States favored slavery.

In 1790, Alexander Hamilton skillfully worked out a compromise between the two factions and a bill was passed to locate the federal city on the Potomac River. President George Washington, who knew the area intimately from his years on his Mount Vernon plantation, was asked by Congress to to determine the exact location for the District of Columbia, and, of course, the capital city was named for him.

The original plans called for exactly 100 square miles to constitute the District of Columbia—a ten-by-ten-mile square taken from the states of

DEDICATION

For Howard and Marion Aylesworth, our best friends in
the Washington area, even though they are relatives.

ACKNOWLEDGMENTS

The author and publisher would like to thank the following
people who helped in the preparation of this book: Elizabeth
Montgomery, who edited it and Mary R Raho, who did the picture research.

Photo Credits

Marcello Bertinetti: 1, 18, 98, 100, 113.
F P G/International: T Algire 30/31; P Beney 36; J Blank 23, 29; B
Buck 66/67; Cezus 41; D Chang 65; F Dole 40; P Gridley 3-6, 45,
46/47, 49, 56/57, 70, 71, 74/75, 80, 104/105, 110/111, 117; D Hallinan
24, 48, 81; J Howard 37, 42/43, 54, 72, 86, 99, 103; M Kaufman 34,
35; V Martin 87; Messerschmidt 53, 115; R P Morrison 114; W
Murphy 58/59; J Neubauer 25, 27; J Pickerell 61, 83; E Powell 82,
126; M Rogers 77; J Scowen 20/21; Stincomb 55; P Weschler 22; W G
Williams 68, 69; Willinger 16, 17; W R Wilson 26, 33, 78/79, 108/109;
H Yaeger 73; E Young 118; J Zehrt 32, 84/85, 94/95; E Zryb 101.
Dennis Krukowski: 76.
Chris Minerva: 50, 92/93, 102.
H Armstrong Roberts: 15, 19, 38/39, 64, 89, 90/91, 96, 97, 106, 107,
116, 119, 120/121, 122, 123, 124/125.
Michael Tamborrino: 51, 52.

and work on the later-built Washington Monument stood still for 20 years—a fact permanently reflected in its two-toned marble facing.

For many years the District development kept well within its original boundaries. In fact, 50 years after its original purchase, Virginia's land was returned, unused, to its original owners. The transaction left the District its present total of 69 square miles, eight of them under water.

In 1814, during the War of 1812, a British Army captured Washington and burned the Capitol, the White House and other government buildings, but the reconstruction of the buildings was completed in 1819. It was then that Washington began growing by leaps and bounds as the demands of government were expanded by war and emergency. From a small town of 40,000 in 1850, it grew to 279,000 in 1900: 802,000 in 1950 and today has a population of a calculated 3,000,000, if one counts the metropolitan area and the 'transient' members of Congress and their staffs.

The first great expansion of the city occurred during the Civil War. Confederate forces kept the capital under virtual siege, and large Union Armies had to be quartered in temporary buildings in the city. In 1871 Congress approved vast improvements to replace these buildings and to improve the appearance of the city.

The second great expansion of the capital came during World War I.

Carpenters hurriedly built ugly temporary buildings along Constitution Avenue to provide office space for additional workers. Some of these buildings still stand.

Washington again increased in size and importance during the Great Depression of the 1930s when greater centralization of the power of the federal government brought in persons from all parts of the country. The government built many new office buildings for the growing federal activities, but even these could not hold all the workers who arrived in Washington during World War II. Government had become big business and a whole new Washington population spilled over into Maryland and Virginia. This expansion continues right into the present time.

Today, Washinton is truly a cosmopolitan city. Perhaps no city on earth has a populace with so many different origins. Representatives from all nations are here: men and women from all of the 50 states work here and vote in their home states by absentee ballot. It is a dignified, distinguished capital, and a beautiful one.

In addition to its functions as a governmental city, Washington is a city of education, with some 11 universities and colleges such as Georgetown University, Catholic University of America and Howard University. It is a city of the arts, with such attractions as the National Gallery of Art, the Hirshhorn Museum and Sculpture Garden, the Freer Gallery of Art, the Corcoran Gallery of Art and the John F Kennedy Center for the Performing Arts. It is a city of sports, with the Redskins of the National Football League, the Bullets of the National Basketball Association, and the Capitals of the National Hockey League. And it is probably the premiere city of museums, with the giant Smithsonian Institution (which includes the National Museums of Natural History, American History, Air and Space, American Art and many more, including the National Zoological Park), the US National Arboretum and various homes and public buildings.

It is the city of the Cherry Blossom Festival, the Georgetown Garden Tour, the Memorial Day Ceremony at the Tomb of the Unknown Soldier in Arlington National Cemetery. It is, above all, the city that makes us all say, 'I'm proud to be an American.'

Thomas G Aylesworth
Virginia L Aylesworth

Capitol Hill

Washington's original planner, Major Pierre Charles L'Enfant, when he started his survey, chose a flat-topped hill as the site of the United States Capitol Building, and this hill is now known as Capitol Hill. The north section of the Capitol was completed in 1800 and Congress held its first session in the building in November that year.

The original plan for the Capitol was drawn by Dr William Thornton of Tortola, West Indies, and accepted 5 April 1793. It had a central section, nearly square, a low dome and rectangular buildings north and south, 126 by 120 feet. The southeast cornerstone of the north section was laid by President Washington with Masonic ceremonies on 18 September 1793. Sandstone from Aquia Creek, Virginia, was used in the construction. The southern wing, however, was completed first, and that is where the Congress first met in 1800, followed by the first meeting of the Supreme Court in February 1801.

The architects in charge of the early construction were Stephen H Hallet, George Hadfield and James Hoban, who was also the architect of the White House. Benjamin H Latrobe was architect of the South, or House Wing, which was occupied in 1807, but not completed until 1811. After the burning by the British in 1814, Latrobe had charge of the rebuilding until 1818, when Charles Bullfinch began his tenure of 11 years as architect. Congress reoccupied the Capitol in 1819 and the central Rotunda area was finished in 1829.

The present Senate and House Wings were designed and constructed from 1851 to 1863 under the architect Thomas U Walter. The wing extensions are white marble from Lee, Massachusetts, and the columns are from Maryland. Daniel Webster spoke at the laying of this cornerstone.

The House of Representatives moved in on 16 December 1857, and the Senate on 4 January 1859. In 1860 the Supreme Court moved into the former Senate Chamber. In 1864 the old Hall of the House was designated Statuary Hall.

The original dome of the Capitol was made of wood covered by copper, but was replaced in 1856 by the present dome of cast iron. The statue of Freedom on the dome was modeled in plaster by Thomas Crawford when he was in Rome and cast in bronze. The cost of the statue was $23,796, exclusive of the cost of erection.

15 An aerial view of the Capitol Building—looking west along the Mall toward the Washington Monument and Lincoln Memorial.

16/17 The setting sun behind the Capitol Building, bathes the Mall and the Washington Monument in shades of red and gold.

18 The interior of the Capitol dome—with its fresco by Constantino Brumidi, entitled the 'Apotheosis of Washington.'

19 The Capitol Building in spring.

20/21 The entrance to the Library of Congress—the National Library. It was established by and for Congress in 1800, and the building dates from 1897.

22 An interior view of the Library of Congress. In 1870 the library became the repository of materials deposited for copyright.

23 The United States Botanic Garden at the foot of Capitol Hill houses a collection of both exotic and familiar plants, plus a fountain designed by the creator of the Statue of Liberty.

24 *The United States Supreme Court Building on Capitol Hill is thought to be the largest building in the world built entirely of marble.*

25 *The enormous statue outside the Supreme Court Building representing 'The Contemplation of Justice' is one of a pair.*

*26 A view of the National Statuary Hall in the
Capitol Building: Ethan Allen, George L Shoup,
King Kamehameha I, and John C Calhoun.*

27 Copies of the original Declaration of Independence, the Constitution and the Bill of Rights are on display in The National Capitol.

The Mall

Originally, Congress had planned to build the buildings that were to accompany the Capitol Building on the high plateau east of Capitol Hill. But land speculators bought most of this land and held out for high prices. In disgust, Congress changed its plans and bought the marshy ground west of the Capitol Building, and this land is now known as The Mall.

The main part of the Mall extends from the United States Capitol to the Washington Monument, and it is a magnificent sweep of green land that is flanked by the myriad of museums that are part of the Smithsonian Institution. It is the heart of Washington and is the main stop on every tourist's trip to the city, where one can be overwhelmed by the majesty of the center of government of the United States at one end and awed by the pinnacle of the monument at the other—with opportunities for edification and entertainment in between.

The Mall reflects the basic plan created by Major L'Enfant, who envisioned a dramatics span of land that would join the 'Congress House' with the beautiful banks of the Potomac River. He wanted to flank the avenue with trees, build a grand canal, and erect seats of learning and entertainment along the edges. But for years nothing happened. Pennsylvania Avenue flourished while shacks and shanties sprang up in the Mall.

It wasn't until the McMillan Plan of 1902 that the government began to think about restoring the Mall as in L'Enfant's original proposal. A railroad was rerouted to a new terminal, Union Station; the Botanic Garden's conservatory was moved to the southeastern edge of the Mall. In the 1970s the Mall's interior streets were transformed into grass and pathways.

The Mall is, however, dominated by the Smithsonian Institution, whose goal is 'the increase and diffusion of knowledge among men.' Surrounding this green oasis are the Smithsonian's Arts and Industries Building, Freer Gallery of Art, Hirshhorn Museum and Sculpture Garden, the National Air and Space Museum, National Gallery of Art, National Museum of Natural History and National Museum of American History. There are other branches of the Smithsonian in other areas of the city, making the Institution truly live up to its nickname—'the nation's attic.'

29 The gorgeously ugly red 'castle,' which is the administration building of the Smithsonian Institution. Inside is the grave of benefactor James Smithson.

30/31 The Smithsonian Institution is one of the world's great historical, scientific, educational and cultural establishments.

32 The statue of George Washington by Horatio Green in the National Museum of American History—a classic example of Greek Revival sculpture.

33 The National Museum of Natural History contains exhibits of gems and minerals, as well as botanical, zoological and geological materials.

34 A nautical display in the Arts and Industries Building. Built between 1879 and 1881, it was originally called The National Museum.

35 One of the sculpture halls in the National
Gallery of Art, a museum that was designed for
the viewer—warm, well-lit and inviting.

36 *The West Building of the National Gallery of Art is one of the world's finest art museums, and was constructed with funds from philanthropist Andrew Mellon.*

37 *Statues displayed outside at the Hirshhorn Museum and Sculpture Garden, built for the late nineteenth and twentieth century art collection of Joseph Hirshhorn.*

38/39 The soaring East Building of the National
Gallery of Art, opened in 1978, was designed by
I M Pei, and is really two triangular buildings.

40 The paleontological exhibit in the National
Museum of Natural History is one of the most
popular in the whole museum.

41 Another favorite display is the Wright Brothers' first airplane in the Smithsonian's National Air and Space Museum.

42/43 The National Air and Space Museum's exhibit of Apollo 10, from which the first lunar landing was accomplished in 1969.

Monuments

The city of Washington is a city of monuments. It seems that no matter where you go, you will find a statue—of a scientist, of a humanitarian, of a philanthropist, of a general or admiral, of a Latin American liberator. And there are other, real, monuments to men of vision, of leadership, of courage.

The dominant one, of course, is the Washington Monument on the Mall. This obelisk is precisely 555 feet 5 1/8 inches high, and is 55 feet square at the base. It is said to be the tallest masonry structure in the world. Sitting in a great green field near Constitution Avenue at the end of the 15th Street Extension, it was opened in 1888 after several construction delays. Most people take the elevator to the top and walk down the 898 spiraled steps to read the carved inscriptions on stones donated by states, foreign countries and organizations.

The capstone of the Washington Monument weighs 3300 pounds and was put in place on 6 December 1884. The Monument was dedicated 21 February 1885 and opened 9 October 1888. The total weight is 81,120 tons. The Monument is dressed with white Maryland marble in two-foot courses, and the first 150 feet are backed by rubble masonry. From that point to 452 feet, Maine granite was used as backing, and above 452 feet, marble was used. The face of the Monument is primarily Maryland marble. The modern elevator ride to the observation level takes one minute, whereas the original elevator ride of 1888 took 12 minutes.

The Lincoln Memorial, built like a Greek temple, faces the Washington Monument across a long reflecting pool. The 19-foot statue of the seated Lincoln by Daniel Chester French looks as though it had been carved from a single block of marble, but it is actually 28 separate pieces. The Memorial, opened in 1922, has the president's Second Inaugural and Gettysburg Addresses inscribed on the walls.

The Jefferson Memorial is the newest of these three, was opened in 1943, while the nation was at war. Pantheon-shaped like his home, Monticello, in Virginia near Charlottesville, it shelters a 19-foot statue, quotations from the Declaration of Independence and other Jefferson documents. It is located at the south end of the Tidal Basin.

45 The Washington Monument on a winter's day.
At 555 feet, it is the tallest structure in the city.

46/47 A view of the Lincoln Memorial (foreground)
and the Washington Monument with the Mall and
the Capitol Building far in the distance.

48 *The statue of Thomas Jefferson, the third President of the United States, in the Jefferson Memorial. The full-length figure was the work of the American sculptor, Rudolph Evans.*

49 *The Jefferson Memorial at Cherry Blossom time. It combines elements of the dome of the Pantheon in Rome with Jefferson's own design for the Rotunda at the University of Virginia.*

50 Visitors come daily to search for the names of loved ones killed in the Vietnam War at the Vietnam Veterans Memorial in Constitution Gardens.

51 The Vietnam Veterans Memorial in its 42-acre
park with flowering trees and a lake, is a V-shaped
black granite memorial designed by Maya Lin,
and lists 57,939 names.

52 A moving tribute to those who died in the Vietnam War is a statue of three American infantrymen located near the Vietnam Veterans Memorial, just across from the Lincoln Memorial.

53 The Lincoln Memorial and its reflecting pool. It is a large Doric temple built of white Colorado-Yule marble with 38 columns.

IN THIS TEMPLE
AS IN THE HEARTS OF THE PEOPLE
FOR WHOM HE SAVED THE UNION
THE MEMORY OF ABRAHAM LINCOLN
IS ENSHRINED FOREVER

54 The heroic statue of Abraham Lincoln in meditation located inside the Lincoln Memorial, sculpted by the Daniel Chester French.

55 Another view of the Lincoln statue in artificial light. Lincoln is seated looking out over Washington's great Mall to the Capitol Building two miles away.

56/57 The Lincoln Memorial. 'In this temple, as in the hearts of the people for whom he saved the Union, the memory of Abraham Lincoln is enshired forever.'

58/59 Nowhere is spring more beautiful than in Washington. Highly cultivated flower gardens fill the area near the Washington Monument.

Downtown and Pennsylvania Avenue

The downtown section of Washington DC is probably the most varied area, with its mix of federal and local government, international organizations, art museums, large department stores, small retail operations, nonprofit organizations and associations, historic sites, parks, hotels, theaters, office buildings, restaurants and bars. Actually, it has been said that the only thing not to be found in downtown Washington is full time residents. At any rate, downtown is certainly where Washingtonians work.

Downtown Washington is also a mecca for the tourist. In the area can be found the National Headquarters of the American Red Cross, the Corcoran Gallery of Art, the DAR's Constitution Hall, the Decatur House, the J Edgar Hoover Building of the FBI, Ford's Theater and the house where Lincoln died, the National Aquarium, the headquarters of the National Geographic Society, the National Museum of American Art, the National Portrait Gallery, the Pan American Union Building, the Renwick Gallery, St John's Church, the Lillian and Albert Small Jewish Museum, the Treasury Building, the Truxton-Decatur Naval Museum, the Washington *Post* and the White House.

In the midst of all this, there is still room for beautiful parks such as Lafayette Square, which is directly across Pennsylvania Avenue from the north entrance to the White House. It began its official life in 1790 as part of the president's front yard in Major L'Enfant's plan for the federal city. But Thomas Jefferson felt that its seven acres would be better used as a public park. Pennsylvania Avenue, the 'Main Street' of the Nation, was cut through in order to separate the square from the White House grounds. Lafayette Square was not officially named until 1824, when it was dedicated to that great friend of the United States, the French Marquis de Lafayette, on the occasion of his final visit to America.

61 The Old Post Office Building on Pennsylvania Avenue at 19th Street has a 315-foot clock tower and dates from the 1890s.

62/63 The White House at night with the Washington Momument in the background. 1600 Pennsylvania Avenue NW is the most prestigious address in the United States.

64 The National Archives houses America's most precious documents, including the Declaration of Independence and the Constitution.

65 The J Edgar Hoover Building houses the headquarters of the United States Federal Bureau of Investigation, a popular tourist attraction.

66/67 When the cherry blossoms appear in late
March or early April, they turn Washington into
a pink and white fairyland.

68 A fanfare is sounded on the White House lawn
to welcome a visiting dignitary to the home of the
president.

69 Street musicians entertaining lunchtime picnickers in Farragut Square. Alfresco dining is popular in downtown Washington in summer.

70/71 Blair House, a graceful mansion dating back to the 1820s, is used to house certain official guests of the president.

72 A station on the Metro—Washington's subway. The Metro was ballyhooed as 'the biggest public works project ever undertaken by man.'

73 Street vendors are a common sight in Washington, especially on Pennsylvania Avenue and around the Mall, where they sell food, souvenirs and other items.

74/75 The wife of President John Adams, Abigail Adams (they were the first residents of the White House), found the building damp and drafty.

76 The Oval Office in the White House is America's seat of power—the private office of the President of the United States.

77 The Lincoln bedroom in the White House has had many famous guests in its time, including Winston Churchill.

78/79 Ford's Theatre with its presidential box— the site of the assassination of Abraham Lincoln by John Wilkes Booth. Lincoln died in a house across the street.

80 The statue of Albert Einstein shows him in a typical pose—relaxed and contemplative—wearing his usual baggy shirt and unpressed trousers.

81 The statue of Andrew Jackson in Lafayette Square is an exact duplicate of Jackson's statue in Jackson Square in New Orleans, and dates from 1853.

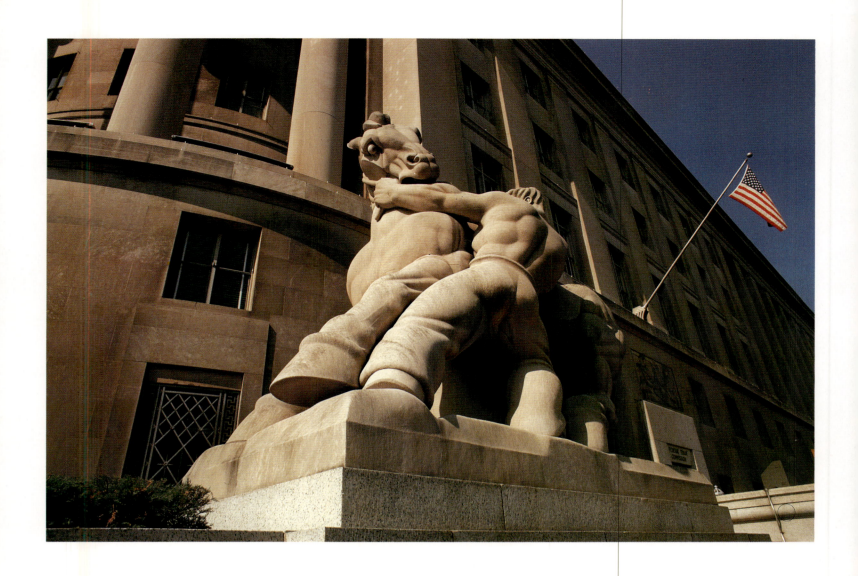

82 The Federal Trade Commission was built in the 1930s in modern classic design, and the statuary is typical of the Art Deco movement of that time.

83 The interior courtyard of the Organization of American States Building (the Pan American Union Building). The patio is filled with tropical plants.

84/85 Pennsylvania Avenue at night, looking toward the lighted facade and dome of the United States Capitol Building.

86 The Metropolitan Club in downtown
Washington DC, one of the most exclusive in the
District of Columbia area.

87 The Nation's Christmas Tree with the Capitol
Building in the background. Each year there is
a ceremony in which the president lights the tree.

Georgetown and the Northwest District

The Northwest District is Washington's largest quadrant and contains much of the city's sightseeing attractions, nightlife, shopping, business and its most prosperous neighborhoods. Along the Gold Coast of 16th Street are many of the city's large beautiful houses as well as scores of embassies, churches and temples.

West of 16th Street and Rock Creek Park are many comfortable neighborhoods, from the Federalist and Victorian houses of Georgetown (which was the social center of the city in the early 1800s) to the luxurious Foxhall Road estates to the turn-of-the-century Cleveland Park houses and newer homes of Chevy Chase. East of 16th Street are more residential areas.

Dupont Circle is on of the most desirable locations in the city and is a center of activity at night. Heading away from Dupont Circle is Massachusetts Avenue—'Embassy Row.' Foggy Bottom is now the location of large government offices.

This district is also the cultural center of Washington. In it are Georgetown University, George Washington University, Howard University and several other institutions of higher learning as well as the John F Kennedy Center for the Performing Arts. The National Zoological Park is there, as is the beautiful Rock Creek Park, with its Nature Center, Art Barn and Carter Barron Amphitheater.

The Northwest District is the home of grand houses of worship. There is the National Presbyterian Church and Center, the New York Avenue Presbyterian Church, Old St John's Church, the National Shrine of the Immaculate Conception, the Franciscan Monastery and the Washington Cathedral.

Then there is Georgetown, which was a flourishing small tobacco port before the District of Columbia was formed. It is, to some, the most charming part of the city, with its narrow streets, cobblestone pathways and old houses.

Georgetown has been called 'Washington's Greenwich Village,' but it is more like London's Chelsea. It is the part of the city with the highest proportion of art galleries, bookstores, quaint shops, fine restaurants and jazz clubs. It also has a number of fine old mansions on its quiet tree-lined streets, with beautiful small secluded gardens behind their tall brick walls.

89 An old brick-sidewalked street in Georgetown with its row of nineteenth century houses—just like a step backward in time.

90/91 The Pierce Mill in Rock Creek Park began grinding grain into flour in the 1820s—corn, wheat, buckwheat and rye.

92/93 The peaceful walkway along the old Chesapeake and Ohio Canal in Georgetown. The canal is over 100 years old.

94/95 The C & O Canal in Georgetown is maintained by the National Park Service and features mule-hauled barges. The canal parallels the Potomac River.

96 The Franciscan Monastery garden contains replicas of great Holy Land shrines, such as the manger at Bethlehem, the Garden of Gethsemane and the Holy Sepulchre.

97 The National Shrine of the Immaculate Conception is the largest Roman Catholic Church in the United States.

98 Music — one of the four statues donated to the people of the United States by the people of Italy, that flank Memorial bridge.

99 The Washington Cathedral is modeled after the great Gothic cathedrals of Europe. It has been under construction since 1907.

100 Robert F Kennedy Stadium, at 22nd and East Capitol Streets, is the home field of the Washington Redskins of the National Football League.

101 The Washington Redskins are a way of life for Washingtonians. Here quarterback Joe Theisman fades back for a pass against the Giants

102 One of the quaint restaurants in Georgetown. Today, Georgetown is one of the most exclusive—and expensive—areas in Washington.

103 A view of Washington DC, seen from across the Potomac at sunset—surely one of the most beautiful cities in the United States.

104/105 The Watergate Complex and the Kennedy Center. Watergate contains expensive apartments, a hotel, exclusive shops and, of course, offices.

106 The small brick houses of Georgetown have been transformed into chic and expensive shops specializing in high fashion clothing and antiques.

107 One of the main attractions at the National Zoological Park is the panda, a gift from the Peoples' Republic of China.

108/109 The John F Kennedy Center for the Performing Arts incorporates an opera house, a concert hall, three theaters and three restaurants.

110/111 A panoramic view of Washington DC showing the White House, the Washington Monument, the Potomac River.

Across the Potomac

The sites across the Potomac from Washington in suburban Virginia are primarily historic or military in nature, and many are associated with the activities of the Washington and Lee families. In Alexandria can be found Robert E Lee's boyhood home, the Lee-Fendall House, the Carlyle House, Gadsby's Tavern and the Stabler-Leadbeater Apothecary, as well as Christ Church. Within 15 miles are Mount Vernon, Woodlawn Plantation and George Washington's Grist Mill, with their rich details of eighteenth century life. In Arlington can be found Arlington National Cemetery, the Iwo Jima Memorial and the Pentagon.

Arlington National Cemetery was originally part of Robert E Lee's estate, and on the grounds is Arlington House (formerly called the Custis-Lee Mansion), as well as the Tomb of the Unknown Soldier, the Memorial Amphitheater and the grave of President John F Kennedy, assassinated 22 November 1963, which is marked with a simple flame.

Alexandria was surveyed by George Washington, and both he and Robert E Lee belonged to Christ Church which was built in 1767 and has been holding services ever since. Washington was also a member of the Friendship Fire Engine Company where today there is an exhibit of early fire-fighting equipment.

Carlyle House is a restored Virginia mansion (1752); the Stabler-Leadbeater Apothecary opened in 1792 and is now a museum; Gadsby's Tavern, built in 1752, was Washington's recruiting headquarters for the French and Indian War and later was a gathering place for Revolutionary leaders. But the most prominent landmark in Alexandria is the George Washington Masonic National Memorial—a 333-foot granite tower.

Nine miles south of Alexandria is Mount Vernon—the plantation of George Washington and one of the most beautiful examples of Colonial architechture in the United States. It is complete with kitchens, dairy, smokehouse, stables, greenhouse, laundry, spinning house, slaves quarters and a small round schoolhouse. Much of the original furniture and many of Washington's possessions—books, letters, swords, clothing (even his false teeth)—are on display. On a hillside near the house is the tomb where George and Martha Washington are buried.

113 The grave of John F Kennedy in Arlington National Cemetery is marked by an eternal flame and quotations from his Inaugural Address.

JOHN FITZGERALD KENNEDY

114 The changing of the guard at the Tomb of the Unknown Soldier in Arlington National Cemetery. The tomb is guarded by elite sentinels of the 3rd US Infantry Regiment.

115 Headstones mark the graves of military dead—those on active service and veterans—in the Arlington National Cemetary. More than 60,000 Americans are buried here including veterans of all the wars.

116 The US Marine Corps War Memorial, formerly known as the Iwo Jima Statue, shows the Marines raising the flag on Iwo Jima during World War II.

117 The terminal at Dulles International Airport was designed in 1962 by the famous architect Eero Saarinen for the most functional airport in the world.

118 The Pentagon, the headquarters of the Department of Defense, is the world's largest office building surrounded by the world's largest parking lot.

119 Queen Street in Old Alexandria, Virginia. Alexandria was established in 1732 by a group of Scottish merchants who built a tobacco warehouse there.

120/121 The City Hall in Alexandria. Alexandria became a town in 1749, when George Washington, the seventeen-year-old assistant to the surveyor John West, laid out the street plan.

122 The Carlyle House in Alexandria, built in 1752 by a Scottish merchant, John Carlyle, was General Braddock's headquarters during the French and Indian War.

123 The Federal parlor of the Lee-Fendall House in Alexandria. It was built in 1785 by Philip Fendall for his second wife, a sister of Light-Horse Harry Lee.

124/125 Mount Vernon. The 5000 acres of land that originally comprised the estate were granted to George Washington's great-grandfather in 1674.